AA Essential

Spanish
for kids

About this book

Jane Wightwick
had the idea

Wina Gunn
wrote the pages

Leila Gaafar (aged 10)
drew the first pictures in
each chapter

Robert Bowers
(not aged 10) drew the
other pictures, and
designed the book

Ana Bremon
did the Spanish stuff

Important things that **must** be included

A CIP catalogue record for this book is available from the British Library

ISBN: 0 7495 2436 7

Published by **AA Publishing** (a trading name of Automobile Association Developments Limited, whose registered office is Millstream, Maidenhead Road, Windsor, Berkshire SL4 5GD. Registered number 1878835)

Printed and bound by **G. Canale & C.S.P.A.**, Torino, Italy

Cover design by **Joshua Smith Graphics**

A01631

3

What's inside

Making friends

How to be cool with the gang

Wanna play?

Our guide to joining in everything from hide-and-seek to the latest electronic game

Feeling hungry

Order your favourite junk or go local

Looking good

Make sure you keep up with all those essential fashions

Hanging out

At the pool, beach or theme park – don't miss out on the action

Pocket money

Spend it here!

Grown-up talk

blah!
blah!
blah!
blah!

If you really, really have to!

Extra bits

All the handy stuff – numbers, months, dates, days of the week

MAKING FRIENDS

me
yo ⟿ yo

my snake
mi serpiente
⟿ mee serpee-entay

my friend
mi amigo
⟿ mee ameego

my friend
mi amiga
⟿ mee ameega

my dog
mi perro
⟿ mee pair-ro

6

my big brother
mi hermano mayor
👄 mee airmano my-yor

grandpa
abuelo
👄 abwelo

grandma
abuela
👄 abwela

dad
papá
👄 pa-pah

mum
mamá
👄 ma-mah

my little sister
mi hermana pequeña
👄 mee airmana pekenya

Half a step this way

stepfather/stepmother
padrastro/madrastra
👄 padrastro/madrastra

stepbrother/
stepsister
hermanastro/
hermanastra
👄 airmanastro/
airmanastra

half-brother/half-sister
medio hermano/medio hermana
👄 medyo airmano/medyo airmana

MAKING FRIENDS

The Spanish put an upside-down question mark before a question, as well as one the right way up at the end. It's the same with exclamation marks.

¿Isn't that weird?   ¡You bet!

Where are you from?
¿De dónde eres?
👄 day donday air-res

from England
de Inglaterra
👄 day eengla-tairra

from Ireland
de Irlanda
👄 day eerlanda

from Scotland
de Escocia
👄 day escothya

from the U.S.
de los Estados Unidos
👄 day los estados ooneedos

from Wales
del País de Gales
👄 del pie-yis day gal-les

That means "the land of the Gauls".

I remember the Gauls. We were always fighting them. Tough nuts to crack!

9

How old are you?
¿Cuántos años tienes?
👄 kwantos anyos tee-enes

12 years old
Doce años
👄 dothay anyos

Happy birthday!
¡Cumpleaños feliz!
👄 koomplay-anyos faileeth

What's your star sign?
¿Qué signo del zodiaco eres?
👄 kay signo del thodee-ako air-res

When's your birthday?
¿Cuándo es tu cumpleaños?
👄 kwando es too koomplay-anyos

Spanish children sing 'Happy Birthday' in Spanish to the same tune. Why don't you practise:

¡Cumpleaños Feliz!
¡Cumpleaños Feliz!

10

Star Signs

AQUARIUS
Jan. 21 – Feb. 19
Acuario 🗫 akwaree-o

PISCES
Feb. 20 – Mar. 20
Piscis 🗫 pees-thees

ARIES
Mar. 21 – Apr. 20
Aries 🗫 a-rees

TAURUS
Apr. 21 – May 21
Tauro 🗫 towro

GEMINI
May 22 – June 21
Géminis 🗫 hemeenees

CANCER
June 22 – July 23
Cáncer 🗫 kanthair

LEO
July 24 – Aug. 23
Leo 🗫 leo

VIRGO
Aug. 24 – Sep. 23
Virgo 🗫 beergo

LIBRA
Sep. 24 – Oct. 23
Libra 🗫 leebra

SCORPIO
Oct. 24 – Nov. 22
Escorpio 🗫 eskorpee-o

SAGITTARIUS
Nov. 23 – Dec. 21
Sagitario 🗫 sa-heetaree-o

CAPRICORN
Dec. 22 – Jan. 20
Capricornio 🗫 kapreecomee-o

12

football
el fútbol
~ el footbol

rollerskating/rollerblading
el patinaje en línea
~ el patee-nahay en leenya

music
la música
~ la mooseeka

electronic games
los juegos electrónicos
~ los hway-gos elektroneekos

tv
la tele
~ la taylay

comics
los tebeos
~ los taybayos

teddies
los ositos de peluche
~ los oseetos day peloochay

school
el colegio
~ el kolay-heeyo

spiders
las arañas
~ las aranyas

13

What's your ...?
Cuál es tu ... ?
🗣 kwal es too ...

favourite group
grupo preferido
🗣 groopo prefereedo

favourite colour
color preferido
🗣 kol-lor prefereedo

 Page 51

favourite food
comida preferida
🗣 komeeda prefereeda

favourite team
equipo preferido
🗣 ekeepo prefereedo

favourite animal
animal preferido
🗣 anee-mal prefereedo

dog
el perro
🗣 el pair-ro

cat
el gato
🗣 el gato

snake
la serpiente
🗣 la serpee-entay

guinea-pig
la cobaya
🗣 la kob-eye-a

hamster
el hámster
🗣 el hamstair

budgie
el periquito
🗣 el peree-keeto

My little doggy goes *guau guau!*

A Spanish doggy (that's "guauguau" in baby language) doesn't say "woof, woof", it says *"guau, guau"* (gwa-oo, gwa-oo). A Spanish bird says *"pío, pío"* (pee-o, pee-o) and "cock-a-doodle-do" in Spanish chicken-speak is *"kikiriki"* (kee-kee ree-kee). But a cat does say *"miaow"* and a cow *"moo"* whether they're speaking Spanish or English!

15

science
las naturales
🗣 las natoorar-les

history
la historia
🗣 la eestoreeya

Way unfair!

Spanish children hardly ever have to wear uniform to school and have very long holidays: 10 weeks in the summer and another 5–6 weeks throughout the rest of the year. But before you turn green with envy, you might not like the mounds of **"deberes para las vacaciones"** (*debaires para las bakathee-yones*), that's "vacation homework"! And if you fail your exams, the teachers could make you repeat the whole year with your little sister!

Gossip

Can you keep a secret?
¿Puedes guardar un secreto?
👄 pwedes gardar oon sekreto

Do you have a boyfriend (a girlfriend)?
¿Tienes novio (novia)?
👄 tee-enes nobyo (nobya)

An OK guy/An OK girl
Un tío majo/Una tía maja
👄 oon teeyo maho/ oona teeya maha

What a bossy-boots!
¡Qué mandón!
👄 kay man-don

He/She's nutty!
¡Está como una cabra!
👄 esta komo oona kabra
That means "He/She's like a goat"!
"I'm not like that at all!"

What a misery-guts!
¡Qué malasombra!
👄 kay malas-sombra

18

You won't make many friends saying this!

Bog off!
¡Vete a la porra!
🗨 betay a la porra

Shut up!
¡Cállate!
🗨 kigh-yatay

If you're fed up with someone, and you want to say something like "you silly …!" or "you stupid …!", you can start with **"pedazo de"** (which actually means "piece of …") and add anything you like. What about …

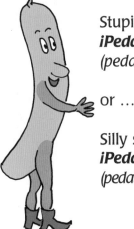

Stupid banana!
¡Pedazo de plátano!
(pedatho day platano)

or …

Silly sausage!
¡Pedazo de salchicha!
(pedatho day salcheecha)

Take your pick. It should do the trick. You could also try **"¡pedazo de idiota!"** (pedatho day eedee-ota). You don't need a translation here, do you?

You might have to say

Bother!
¡Ostras!
os-stras

Rats!
¡Porras!
porras

"Did someone call us?"

las ostras →

I'm fed up
Estoy harto! (boys)
Estoy harta! (girls)
estoy arto
estoy arta

That's enough!
¡Ya vale!
ya balay

I don't care
Me da igual
may da igwal

Stop it!
¡Para!
para

At last!
¡Por fin!
por feen

20

Saying goodbye

What's your address?
¿Cuál es tu dirección?
🗨 kwal es too deerek-thyon

Here's my address
Aquí tienes mi dirección
🗨 akee tee-enes mee deerek-thyon

Come to visit me
Ven a visitarme
🗨 ben a beesee-tarmay

Write to me soon
Escríbeme pronto
🗨 escree-bemay pronto

Have a good trip!
¡Buen viaje!
🗨 bwen bee-ahay

Bye!
¡Adiós!
🗨 adeeyos

21

WANNA PLAY?

el elástico
👄 el elasteeko

el ping-pong
👄 el "ping-pong"

el avión
👄 el abee-on

el Gameboy®
👄 el "gameboy"

las canicas
👄 las kaneekas

el yo-yó
👄 el "yo yo"

WANNA PLAY?

23

Not now.
Ahora no
👄 a-ora no

Yeah!
¡Vale!
👄 balay

Fancy a game of **foal** or **donkey**?!

In Spain, you don't play "leap frog", you play "foal" – *el potro*. There is also a group version of this called "donkey" – *el burro*. This involves two teams. Team 1 line up in a row with their heads down in the shape of a donkey. Team 2 take it in turns to leap as far as they can onto the back of the "donkey". If the donkey falls over, Team 2 win. If Team 2 touch the ground or can't leap far enough to get all the team on, then Team 1 win – got that?! Spanish children will try to tell you this is enormous fun, but your parents might not be so keen on the bruises!

Make yourself heard

Electronic games

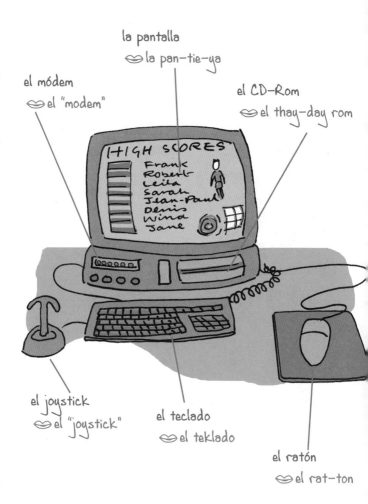

la pantalla
👄 la pan-tie-ya

el módem
👄 el "modem"

el CD-Rom
👄 el thay-day rom

HIGH SCORES
Frank
Robert
Leila
Sarah
Jean-Paul
Denis
Wind
Jane

el joystick
👄 el "joystick"

el teclado
👄 el teklado

el ratón
👄 el rat-ton

28

What do I do?
¿Qué hay que hacer?
👄 kay eye kay athair

Show me
Enséñame
👄 ensay-nyamay

Am I dead?
¿Me han matado?
👄 may an matado

Shoot-em-up!
¡Dispárales!
👄 deespar-ralayz

How many lives do I have?
¿Cuántas vidas tengo?
👄 kwantas beedas tengo

How many levels are there?
¿Cuántos niveles hay?
👄 kwantos neebay-les eye

Non couch-potato activities!

tennis
el tenis
👄 el tenees

trampolining
el trampolín
👄 el "trampoline"

bowling
los bolos
👄 los bol-los

swimming
la natación
👄 la nata-thyon

hockey
el hockey
👄 el "hockey"

gymnastics
la gimnasia
👄 la heem-nasya

basketball   el baloncesto
👄 el ballon-thesto

ballet
el ballet
👄 el ballay

and, of course, we haven't forgotten *"el fútbol"* … (P.T.O.)

footy

boots
las botas
👄 las botas

shin-pads
las espinilleras
👄 las espinee-yeras

ref
el árbitro
el arbeetro

football kit
el equipo de fútbol
👄 el ekeepo day footbol

Good save!
¡Vaya parada!
👄 baya parada

crossbar
el larguero
👄 el largairo

goalpost
el palo
👄 el pallo

goal
el gol
👄 el gol

goalie
el portero
👄 el portairo

Pass!
¡Pasa!
👄 pasa

33

Showing off

... do a handstand?
... hacer el pino?
👄 athair el peeno

Can you ...
¿Sabes ...
👄 sabays

Look at me!
¡Mírame!
👄 meera-may

... do a cartwheel?
... dar volteretas laterales?
👄 dar boltair-retas latairal-les

... do this?
... hacer esto?
👄 athair esto

Impress your Spanish friends with this!

You can show off to your new Spanish friends by practising this tongue twister:

Tres tristes tigres comían trigo en un trigal

trays treestays teegrays comee-an treego en oon treegal

(This means "Three sad tigers ate wheat in a wheat field".)

Then see if they can do as well with this English one:
"She sells sea shells on the sea shore, but the shells she sells aren't sea shells, I'm sure."

For a rainy day

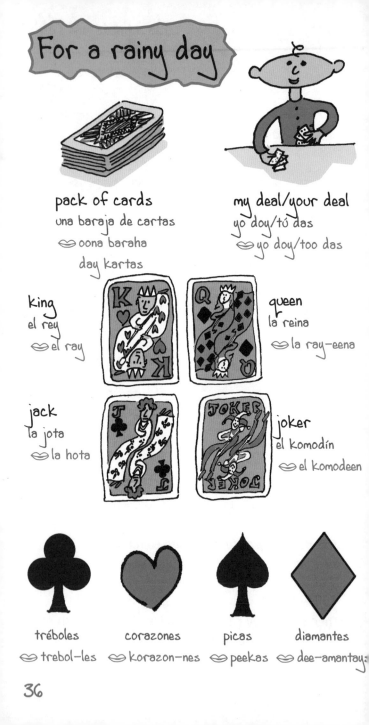

pack of cards
una baraja de cartas
oona baraha
day kartas

my deal/your deal
yo doy/tú das
yo doy/too das

king
el rey
el ray

queen
la reina
la ray-eena

jack
la jota
la hota

joker
el komodín
el komodeen

tréboles
trebol-les

corazones
korazon-nes

picas
peekas

diamantes
dee-amantay:

Do you have the ace of swords?!

You might also see Spanish children playing with a different pack of cards. There are only 48 cards instead of 52 and the suits are also different. Instead of clubs, spades, diamonds and hearts, there are gold coins (**oros**), swords (**espadas**), cups (**copas**) and batons (**bastos**).

chessboard
el tablero
🗣 el tablairo

el alfil
🗣 el alfeel

el caballo
🗣 el kab-eye-o

el peón
🗣 el pay-on

la torre
🗣 la torray

la reina
🗣 la ray-eena

el rey
🗣 el ray

37

FEELING HUNGRY

hamburger
la hamburguesa
🗨 la amboorgaysa

chips
las patatas fritas
🗨 las patatas
freetas

ice-cream
el helado
🗨 el elardo

coke
una coca
🗨 oona koka

creme caramel
el flan
👄 el flan
(Watch out! "Flan" in Spanish doesn't mean a pastry tart with cheese!)

squid
los calamares
👄 los kalamar-res

la paella
👄 la pie-eyya

orange juice
el zumo de naranja
👄 el thoomo day naran-ha

FEELING HUNGRY

39

Grub

I'm starving
Tengo un hambre de lobo
👄 tengo oon ambray day lobo

That means
"I have the
hunger of a wolf!"

el lobo

Please can I have ...
Por favor, me da ...
👄 por fabor, may da

... **a cream bun**
un bollo con nata
👄 oon boyo kon nata

... **a croissant**
un cruasán
👄 oon krwasan

... **a puff pastry**
una palmera
👄 oona palmayra

40

... a muffin
una magdalena
👄 oona magda-layna

... a waffle
un gofre
👄 oon go-fray

los churros
👄 los choorros

These are wonderful sugary doughnut-like snacks. They are sold in cafés and kiosks and usually come in a paper cone. They are also very popular for breakfast in winter, with thick hot chocolate (*chocolate con churros*).

You: Can I have some churros, Mum?

Mum: No. They'll make you fat and rot your teeth.

You: But I think it's good to experience a foreign culture through authentic local food.

Mum: Oh, all right then.

Churros? *"¡Mm, mm!"*, Garlic sandwich? *"¡Agh!"*. If you're going to make foody noises you'll need to know how to do it properly in Spanish!

"Yum, yum!" is out in Spanish. You should say *"¡Mm, mm!"*. And "Yuk!" is *"¡Agh!"* (pronounced "ag"), but be careful not to let adults hear you say this!

Drink up

I'm dying for a drink
Me muero de sed
👄 may mwero day sed

I'd like ...
Me apetece ...
👄 may apay–tethay

... a coke
... una coca
👄 oona koka

... an orange juice
... un zumo de naranja
👄 oon thoomo day naran–ha

... an apple juice
... un zumo de manzana
👄 oon thoomo day manthana

42

In Spain ask for **una Fanta® de limón** when you want a lemonade or **Fanta® de naranja** (*fanta day naran-ha*) for a fizzy orange. Fanta® is the most popular type and so that's what people say.

... a lemonade
una Fanta®
de limón
🗨 oona Fanta
day leemon

... water
agua
🗨 agwa

... a milkshake
... un batido
🗨 oon bateedo

You get your hot chocolate in a large cup (to dunk your churros in).

... a hot chocolate
... un chocolate
🗨 oon chokolatay

Did you know?

A lot of children have hot chocolate for breakfast in the morning and some of them will dip their churros or muffins in it. They go all soggy and Mum is sure not to like this!

43

Tap into *Tapas*

There's a perfect way to try a little bit of everything in Spain and that's "*tapas*". These are little snacks that everyone eats in cafés and bars (which the adults might insist on going to).

Tapas come in little dishes and are a great way of finding out if you like something without risking a torrent of abuse if you leave an expensive meal untouched.

Here are four of the most popular:

tortilla

👄 tortee-ya

Spanish omelette – thick and comes in slices

croquetas

👄 kroketas

egg-shaped rissoles filled with chicken, ham or fish

albóndigas

👄 albon-deegas

meatballs in tomato sauce

calamares a la romana

👄 kalamar-res a la romana

squid rings

L O O K I N G   G O O D

nail varnish
la pintura de uñas
🗣 la peentoora day oonyas

headband
la diadema
🗣 la dee-adema

braid
la trencita
🗣 la tren-theeta

bracelets
las pulseras
🗣 las poolsairas

crop top
la camiseta
🗣 la kameeset

belt
el cinturón
🗣 el theen-tooron

miniskirt
la minifalda
🗣 la minee-falda

shoes
los zapatos
🗣 los thapatos

bike
la bici
🗣 la beethee

46

cap
la gorra
🗣 la gorra

T-shirt
la camiseta
🗣 la kameeseta

tatoo
la calcamonía
🗣 la kalka–moneeya

jeans
los vaqueros
🗣 los bakayros

el walkman
🗣 el "walkman"

skateboard
el monopatín
🗣 el mono–pateen

trainers
las deportivas
🗣 las daypor–teebas

LOOKING GOOD

47

That T-shirt please
Esa camiseta, por favor
👄 esa kameeseta, por fabor

Cool tattoo!
¡Qué calcamonía más chula!
👄 kay kalka-moneeya mass choola

The pink frilly one
La rosa con volantitos
👄 la rosa kon bolanteetos

A braid, please
Una trencita, por favor
👄 oona trentheeta, por fabor

The purple stripey one
La morada de rayas
👄 la morada day righ-yas

Awesome miniskirt!
¡Vaya minifalda mas chula!
👄 baya meenee falda mass choola

Where's my skateboard?
¿Dónde está mi monopatín?
👄 donday esta mee mono-pateen

A pair of cowboys?

The word for jeans in Spanish (*los vaqueros* – *los bakayros*) actually means "cowboys" because they were the first people to wear these trousers.

48

spotty
de lunares
👄 day loonar-res

flowery
de flores
👄 day flor-res

frilly
con volantitos
👄 kon bolanteetos

glittery
con brillos
👄 kon breeyos

stripey
de rayas
👄 day righ-yas

jeans
los vaqueros
😊 los bakayros

T-shirt
la camiseta
😊 la kameeseta

sweatshirt
la sudadera
😊 la sooda-dayra

trainers
las deportivas
😊 las daypor-teebas

dress
el traje
😊 el trahay

trousers
los pantalones
😊 los panta-lone-nes

skirt
la falda
😊 la falda

football shirt
la camiseta de fútbol
😊 la kameeseta day footbol

shorts
los pantalones cortos
😊 los panta-lone-nes kortos

shoes
los zapatos
😊 los thapatos

50

Colour this page yourself
(you can't expect us to do everything!)

colours
los colores
👄 los kolor-res

white
blanco
👄 blanko

green
verde
👄 berday

orange
naranja
👄 naranha

blue
azul
👄 athool

pink
rosa
👄 roza

yellow
amarillo
👄 amareeyo

red
rojo
👄 roho

black
negro
👄 negro

purple
morado
👄 morado

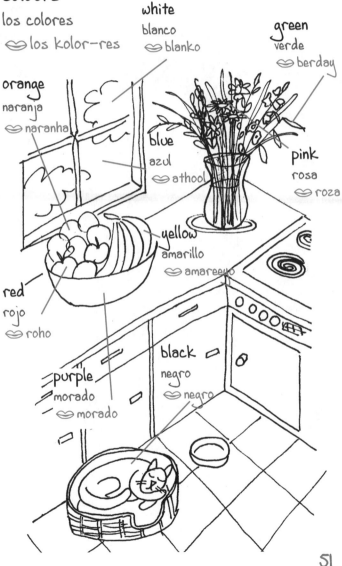

51

What shall we do?
¿Qué hacemos?
👄 kay athay-mos

Can I come?
¿Puedo ir?
👄 pwedo eer

Where do you lot hang out?
¿Por dónde salís vosotros?
👄 por donday salees bos-otros

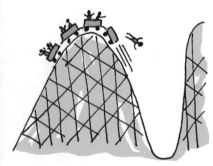

That's really wicked
Eso es chachi
👄 eso es chachee

I'm (not) allowed
(No) me dejan
👄 (no) may day-han

Let's go back
Regresemos
👄 regray-saymos

That gives me goose bumps (or "chicken flesh" in Spanish!)
Eso me pone la carne de gallina
👄 eso may ponay la karnay day galyeena

I'm scared
Tengo miedo
👄 tengo mee-aydo

I'm bored to death
Me muero de aburrimiento
👄 may mwero day aburree-mee-ento

That's a laugh
Te ríes cantidad
👄 tay reeyes kanteedad

55

Beach babies

Can I borrow this?
¿Me dejas esto?
👄 may dehas esto

Let's hit the beach
¿Vamos a la playa?
👄 bamos a la playa

Is this your bucket?
¿Es tuyo este cubo?
👄 es tooyo estay koobo

You can bury me
Me puedes enterrar
👄 may pwedes entair-rar

Stop throwing sand!
¡Deja de echar arena!
👄 dayha day echar arayna

Mind my eyes!
¡Cuidado con mis ojos!
👄 kweedado kon mees ohos

sea
el mar
👄 el mar

beach
la playa
👄 la playa

sandcastle
el castillo de arena
👄 el casteeyo day arayna

towel
la toalla
👄 la toe-aya

swimming costume
el bañador
👄 el banyador

bucket
el cubo
👄 el koobo

snorkel
el tubo
👄 el toobo

shells
las conchas
👄 las konchas

spade
la pala
👄 la palla

57

It's going swimmingly!

How to make a splash in Spanish!

P L O F

Let's hit the swimming pool
Vamos a la piscina
👄 bamos a la peeseena

Can you swim (underwater)?
¿Sabes nadar (debajo del agua)?
👄 sabays nadar (debaho del agwa)

Me too/ I can't
Yo también/Yo no
👄 yo tambeeyen/ yo no

Can you dive?
¿Te sabes tirar de cabeza?
👄 tay sabays teerar day kabaytha

I'm getting changed
Me estoy cambiando
👄 may estoy kambee-ando

58

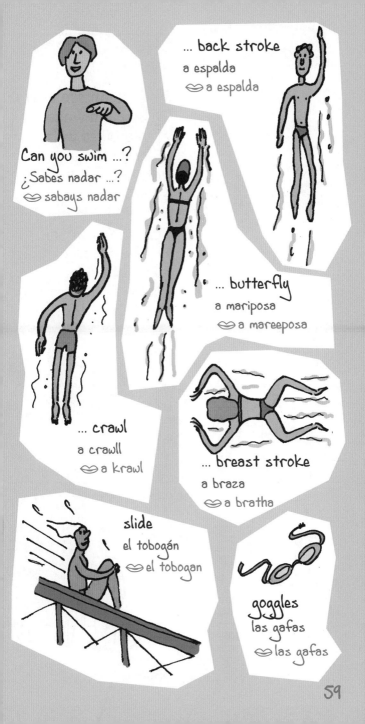

... back stroke
a espalda
👄 a espalda

Can you swim ...?
¿Sabes nadar ...?
👄 sabays nadar

... butterfly
a mariposa
👄 a mareeposa

... crawl
a crawll
👄 a krawl

... breast stroke
a braza
👄 a bratha

slide
el tobogán
👄 el tobogan

goggles
las gafas
👄 las gafas

59

Do you know the way?
¿Te sabes el camino?
🗨 tay sabays el kameeno

Is it far?
¿Está lejos? 🗨 esta lay-hos

Pooper-scoopers on wheels!

You might see bright green-and-white motorbikes with funny vacuum cleaners on the side riding around town scooping up the dog poop. The people riding the bikes look like astronauts! (Well, you'd want protection too, wouldn't you?)

Are we allowed in here?
¿Nos dejan entrar aquí?
🗨 nos day-han entrar akee

Let's ask
Vamos a preguntar
🗨 bamos a pray-goontar

60

playground
el patio de recreo
🗨 el pateeyo day rekrayo

slide
el tobogán
🗨 el tobogan

swings
los columpios
🗨 los koloom-peeyos

park
el parque
🗨 el parkay

bus
el autobús
🗨 el owtoboos

car
el coche
🗨 el kochay

You could gain a lot of street cred with your new Spanish friends by using a bit of slang. A clapped-out car is *"una cafetera"* (*oona cafaytayra*), which means "coffee pot"! Try this: *"¡Vaya cafetera!"* (*baya cafaytayra* – "What an old banger!").

61

Picnics

I hate wasps
Odio las avispas
~ odeeyo las abeespas

Move over!
¡Apártate!
~ apar–tatay

bread
el pan
~ el pan

Let's sit here
¿Nos sentamos aquí?
~ nos sentamos akee

napkin
la servilleta
~ la serbeeyeta

ham
el jamón
~ el hamon

cheese
el queso
~ el kayso

yoghurt
el yogurt
~ el yogurt

crisps
las patatas fritas
~ las patatas freetas

drinks
las bebidas
👄 las bedeedas

knife
el cuchillo
👄 el koocheeyo

spoon
la cuchara
👄 la koochara

fork
el tenedor
👄 el tenaydor

wasps
las avispas
👄 las abeespas

bees
las abejas
👄 las abayhas

bzzzz

ants
las hormigas
👄 las ormeegas

All the fun of the fair

helter-skelter
el tobogán
🗣️ el tobogan

big wheel
la noria
🗣️ la noreeya

house of mirrors
la casa de los espejos
🗣️ la kasa day los espayhos

dodge-ems
los coches de choque
🗣️ los kochays day chokay

Let's go on this
¿Nos montamos en éste?
🗣️ nos montamos en estay

roundabout
el pulpo
🔊 el poolpo

It's (too) fast
Va muy rápido
🔊 ba mwee rapeedo

That's for babies
eso es para los pequeños
🔊 eso es para los
pekay-nyos

Do you get wet in here?
¿En éste te mojas?
🔊 en estay tay mohas

I'm not going on my own
Yo solo no me monto
🔊 yo solo no may monto

65

Spend it here

sweets
los caramelos
👄 los karamaylos

T-shirts
las camisetas
👄 las kameesetas

POCKET MONEY

toys
los juguetes
👄 los hoogetes

el tendero
👄 el tendayro

books
los libros
🗣 los leebros

el móvil
🗣 el mobeel

pencils
los lápices
🗣 los lapeethes

POCKET MONEY

What does that sign say?

carnicería
butcher shop
↪ karneethereeya

pastelería
cake shop
↪ pasteler-
reeya

panadería
bakery
↪ panadereeya

confitería
sweet shop
↪ confeeter-
reeya

papelería
stationers
↪ papelereeya

verdulería
grocery shop
↪ berdooler-
reeya

boutique
clothes shop
↪ booteek

Money talk

Money in Spain is the **euro** (pay attention – you may be spending it at home soon!).

Coins: 1, 2, 5, 10, 20, 50 **euro cents**; and 1, 2 **euro.**

Notes: 5, 10, 20, 50, 100, 200, 500 **euro**

Make sure you know how much you're spending before you blow all your pocket money in one go!

69

Sweet heaven!

I love this shop
Me encanta esta tienda
☞ may enkanta esta tee-enda

Let's get some sweets
Vamos a comprar chucherías
☞ bamos a comprar choochereeyas

Let's get an ice cream
Vamos a por un helado
☞ bamos a por oon elado

lollipops
las piruletas
☞ las peerooletas

a bar of chocolate
una tableta de chocolate
☞ oona tableta day chokolatay

chewing gum
el chicle
☞ el cheeklay

If you really want to look Spanish and end up with lots of fillings ask for:

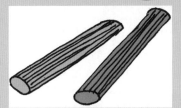

regaleez
(regaleeth)

soft licorice sticks, available in red or black

nubes (noobes)

soft marshmallow sweets ("flumps") in different shades (**nubes** means clouds)

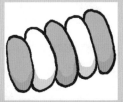

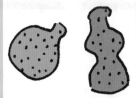

jamones
(hamon-nes)

fruity, fizzy gums in the shape of hams ("ham" is **jamón**)

Chupa-chups® (choopa-choops)

lollies famous all over the world, but they come from Spain

polvos pica-pica (polvos pika pika)

tangy fizzy sherbet sold in small packets with a lollipop to dip in

kilométrico (keelomay-treeko)

chewing gum in a strip like dental floss – pretend to the adults that you're flossing your teeth!

Other things you could buy

(that won't rot your teeth!)

What are you getting?
¿Qué te vas a comprar?
👄 kay tay bas a komprar

That toy, please
Ese juguete, por favor
👄 esay hoogetay, por fabor

Two postcards, please
Dos postales, por favor
👄 dos postal-
les, por fabor

How much is that?
¿Cuánto cuesta?
👄 kwanto kwesta

This is rubbish
Esto es una porquería
👄 esto es oona
porkayreeya

This is cool
Esto mola
👄 esto mola

... colouring pencils
... lápices de colores
~ lapeethes day kolor-res

I'm getting ...
Voy a comprar ~ boy a comprar

... stamps
... sellos
~ seyos

... felt tip pens
... rotuladores
~ rotoolador-res

... a pen
... un boli
~ oon bolee

... a cassette
... una cinta
~ oona theenta

... a CD
... un compact
~ oon compact

... comics
... tebeos
~ taybayos

For many years Spain's favourite comics have been *Mortadelo y Filemón*, two accident-prone TIA agents (<u>not</u> CIA) and *Zipi y Zape*, two very naughty twins. Children also like to read *Mafalda*, an Argentinian comic, *Carlitos y Snoopy* (Charlie Brown & Snoopy), *Tintin*, *Astérix* and *¿Dónde está Wally?* (Where's Wally?).

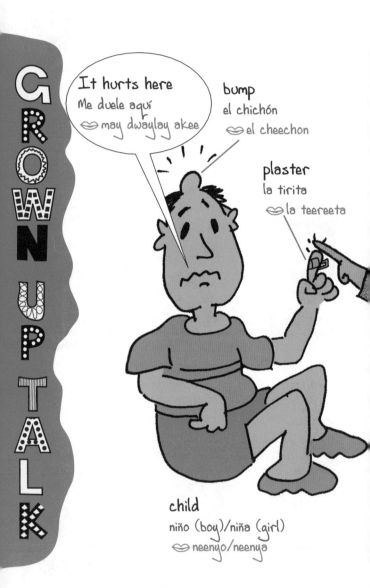

75

Help!

Something has dropped/broken
Algo se ha caído/roto
algo say a kigh-eedo/roto

Please
Por favor
por fabor

Can you help me?
¿Me puedes ayudar?
may pwedes ayoodar

Where's the letter box?
¿Dónde está el buzón?
donday esta el boothon

Where are the toilets?
¿Dónde están los aseos?
donday estan los asayos

I can't manage it
No puedo
👄 no pwedo

Could you pass me that?
¿Me pasas eso?
👄 may pasas eso

What's the time?
¿Qué hora es?
👄 kay ora es

Come and see
Ven a ver
👄 ben a bair

May I look on your watch?
¿Me deja que mire su reloj?
👄 may deha kay meera soo reloh

77

Lost for words

... my ticket
mi billete
💬 mee biyetay

I've lost ...
He perdido ...
💬 eh perdeedo

... my bike
mi bici
💬 mee beethee

... my parents
mis padres
💬 mees padrays

... **my shoes**
mis zapatos
👄 mees thapatos

... **my money**
mi dinero
👄 mee deenayro

... **my jumper**
mi jersey
👄 mee hersay

... **my watch**
mi reloj
👄 mee reloh

... **my jacket**
mi chaqueta
👄 mee chaketa

79

ADULTS ONLY!

Show this page to adults who can't seem to make themselves clear (it happens). They will point to a phrase, you read what they mean and you should all understand each other perfectly.

No te preocupes
Don't worry

Siéntate aquí
Sit down here

¿Tu nombre y apellidos?
What's your name and surname?

¿Cuántos años tienes?
How old are you?

¿De dónde eres?
Where are you from?

¿Dónde te alojas?
Where are you staying?

¿Dónde te duele?
Where does it hurt?

¿Eres alérgico a algo?
Are you allergic to anything?

Está prohibido
It's forbidden

Tiene que acompañarte un adulto
You have to have an adult with you

Voy a por alguien que hable inglés
I'll get someone who speaks English

Knock, knock.

Who's there?

Uno.

Uno who?

Unos where I got this crummy joke!

uno   👄 oono

dos   👄 dos

tres   👄 trays

cuatro   👄 kwatro

cinco   👄 theenko

seis ➰ sayis

siete ➰ see-etay

ocho ➰ ocho

nueve ➰ nwebay

diez ➰ deeyeth

once ➰ onthay

doce ➰ dothay

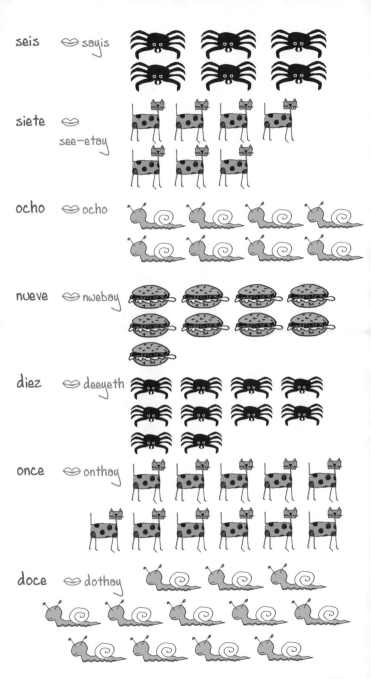

13	trece	*trethay*
14	catorce	*katorthay*
15	quince	*keenthay*
16	dieciséis	*deeyethee sayis*
17	diecisiete	*deeyethee see-etay*
18	dieciocho	*deeyethee ocho*
19	diecinueve	*deeyethee nwebay*
20	veinte	*baintay*

I f you want to say "twenty-two", "sixty-five" and so on, you can just put the two numbers together like you do in English. But don't forget to add the word for "and" (**y** – *ee*) in the middle:

32	**treinta y dos**	*traynta ee dos*
54	**cincuenta y cuatro**	*theenkwenta ee kwatro*
81	**ochenta y uno**	*ochenta ee oono*

30	treinta	*traynta*
40	cuarenta	*kwarenta*
50	cincuenta	*theenkwenta*
60	sesenta	*saysenta*
70	setenta	*saytenta*
80	ochenta	*ochenta*
90	noventa	*nobenta*
100	cien	*theeyen*

1st	primero	*preemairo*
2nd	segundo	*segoondo*
3rd	tercero	*terthayro*
4th	cuarto	*kwarto*
5th	quinto	*keento*
6th	sexto	*sexto*
7th	séptimo	*septeemo*
8th	octavo	*octabo*
9th	noveno	*nobayno*
10th	décimo	*daytheemo*

Fancy a date?

If you want to say a date in Spanish, you don't need to use 1st, 2nd, etc. Just say

Lunes	Martes	Miércoles	Jueves	Viernes	Sábado	Domingo
		1	2	3	4	5
6	7	8	9	10	11	12
13	14	15	16	17	18	19
20	21	22	23	24	25	26
27	28	29	30			

the ordinary number followed by *de* (*day*):

uno de marzo   (1st of March)

diez de Julio   (10th of July)

March	marzo	*martho*
April	abril	*abreel*
May	mayo	*my-yo*

June	junio	*hooneeyo*
July	julio	*hooleeyo*
August	agosto	*agosto*

September	septiembre	*septee-embray*
October	octubre	*octoobray*
November	noviembre	*nobee-embray*

December	diciembre	*deethee-embray*
January	enero	*enayro*
February	febrero	*febrayro*

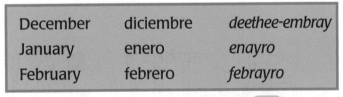

primavera *preemabayra*

verano *berano*

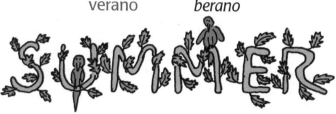

otoño *otonyo*

autumn

invierno *eenbee-erno*

Monday	lunes	*loon-nes*
Tuesday	martes	*mar-tes*
Wednesday	miércoles	*mee-erkol-les*
Thursday	jueves	*hoo-ebes*
Friday	viernes	*bee-er-nes*
Saturday	sábado	*sabado*
Sunday	domingo	*domeengo*

By the way, Spanish kids have a two-and-a-half hour lunch break! Time enough for lunch and a siesta. But they don't finish until 5pm in the afternoon.

Good times

It's ...
Son ...
🗣 sonn

(five) o'clock
las (cinco)
🗣 las (theenko)

quarter past (two)
las (dos) y cuarto
🗣 las (dos) ee kwarto

quarter to (four)
las (cuatro) menos cuarto
🗣 las (kwatro) menos kwarto

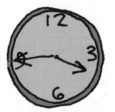

half past (three)
las (tres) y media
🗣 las (trays) ee medya

five past (ten)
las (diez) y cinco
🗣 las (deeyeth) ee theenko

twenty past (eleven)
las (once) y veinte
🗣 las onthay ee baintay

ten to (four)
las (cuatro) menos diez
🗣 las (kwatro) menos deeyeth

twenty to (six)
las (seis) menos veinte
🗣 las sayis menos baintay

Watch out for "one o'clock". It's a bit different from the other times. If you want to say "It's one o'clock" you have to say **_Es la una_** (*es la oona*). "It's half past one" is **_Es la una y media_** (*es la oona ee medya*), and so on.

morning
mañana
🗣 la manyarna

midday
mediodía
🗣 el medyo-deeya

afternoon
la tarde
🗣 la tarday

midnight
la medianoche
🗣 la medya-nochay

evening
la noche
🗣 la nochay

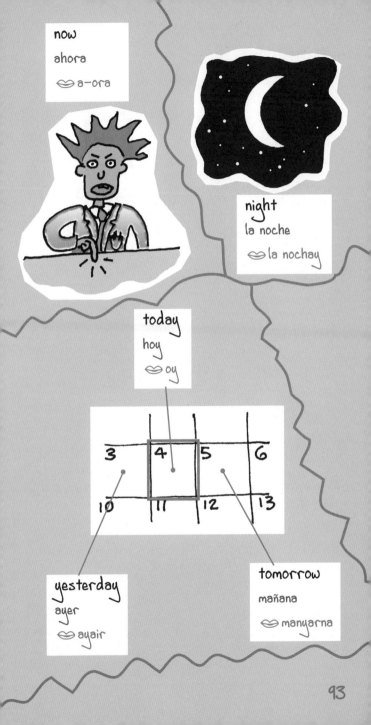

now
ahora
👄 a-ora

night
la noche
👄 la nochay

today
hoy
👄 oy

3 4 5 6
10 11 12 13

yesterday
ayer
👄 ayair

tomorrow
mañana
👄 manyarna

93

Weather wise

Can we go out?
¿Podemos salir fuera?
 podaymos saleer fwera

It's hot
Hace calor
athay kalor

It's cold
Hace frío
athay freeyo

It's a horrible day
Hace un día horrible
athay oon deeya orreeblay

It's raining seas!

In Spanish it doesn't rain "cats and dogs", it rains "seas"! That's what they say when it's raining really heavily:

¡Está lloviendo a mares! *esta yobeeyendo a mar-res*

It's windy
Hace viento
≋ athay beeyento

It's sunny
Hace sol
≋ athay sol

It's raining
Está lloviendo
≋ esta yobeeyendo

It's snowing
Está nevando
≋ esta nebando

I'm soaked
Estoy empapado
≋ estoy empapardo

It's nice
Hace bueno
≋ athay bweno

95